De
V
g...
d

Illustrated by Clare Els

Raintree is an imprint of Capstone Global Library Limited, a company incorporated in England and Wales having its registered office at 7 Pilgrim Street, London, EC4V 6LB – Registered company number: 6695582

www.raintreepublishers.co.uk
myorders@raintreepublishers.co.uk

Text © Capstone Global Library Limited 2013
First published in hardback in 2013
Paperback edition first published in 2014
The moral rights of the proprietor have been asserted.

Edited by Dan Nunn, Rebecca Rissman, and
 Catherine Veitch
Designed by Philippa Jenkins
Original illustrations © Clare Elsom
Illustrated by Clare Elsom
Production by Victoria Fitzgerald
Originated by Capstone Global Library Ltd
Printed and bound in China

ISBN 978 1 406 25045 9 (hardback)
16 15 14 13 12
10 9 8 7 6 5 4 3 2 1

ISBN 978 1 406 25055 8 (paperback)
17 16 15 14
10 9 8 7 6 5 4 3 2 1

British Library Cataloguing in Publication Data
Thomas, Isabel.
Worried. -- (Dealing with Feeling...)
152.4'6-dc23
A full catalogue record for this book is available from the British Library.

Every effort has been made to contact copyright holders of material reproduced in this book. Any omissions will be rectified in subsequent printings if notice is given to the publisher.

All the Internet addresses (URLs) given in this book were valid at the time of going to press. However, due to the dynamic nature of the Internet, some addresses may have changed, or sites may have changed or ceased to exist since publication. While the author and publisher regret any inconvenience this may cause readers, no responsibility for any such changes can be accepted by either the author or the publisher.

Contents

Some words are shown in bold, **like this.** Find out what they mean in the glossary on page 23.

What is worry?

Worry is a **feeling**. It is normal to have many kinds of feelings every day.

Some feelings are not nice to have. Worry is not a nice feeling. We feel worried when we think something bad might happen.

What does it feel like to be worried?

TEST

Sometimes we might feel worried for a short time. When you are **nervous**, it can feel like there are butterflies in your tummy.

Sometimes worries can be very strong, and last for a long time. It can be difficult to stop thinking about them.

How do we know when someone is worried?

Our faces and bodies can show other people how we are feeling. Also, we may show how we are feeling in the way that we behave.

Some people are grumpy when they
are worried, even with their friends.
Other people try to hide their worries.
This can make them feel worse.

Is it normal to feel worried?

Some changes are exciting. Others can make you feel worried. It is normal to feel worried about a big change, such as moving to a new house or school.

If you do something that you enjoy it might stop you worrying.

How can I deal with worries?

Sometimes things you see on the internet or television can make you feel scared. It can be hard to deal with worries on your own.

Ask a grown-up to **explain** what you have seen. Finding out more about something can make it feel less scary.

Why is it good to share my worries?

When somebody in your family gets ill, it can make you feel very worried. Talking about your worries can make you feel better.

A grown-up can help you understand what is going on. Sometimes the thoughts inside our heads are very different from what is really happening.

What if I can't talk about my feelings?

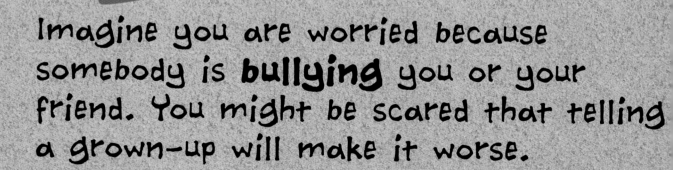

Imagine you are worried because somebody is **bullying** you or your friend. You might be scared that telling a grown-up will make it worse.

Other times, it is hard to put **feelings** into words. Try drawing a picture of your worries instead, and show it to a grown-up whom you trust.

Why should I deal with worries?

Keeping worries inside can make you feel worse. Worries can get in the way and can stop you from enjoying fun things.

You might not be able to **concentrate** at school. The best way to deal with **feelings** is to talk about them.

How can I help someone who is feeling worried?

Everyone feels worried sometimes, even grown-ups. When people you know are worried, they might want to talk about how they feel.

You can help by listening. Sometimes, just sharing worries with someone makes the worries go away.

Make a worry toolbox

Write down some tips to help you deal with worried **feelings.**

Find out more about the thing that is worrying you.

Take your mind off worrying by reading a book or listening to music.

Try to think happy thoughts.

Take a few deep breaths.

Go for a walk or a run.

Share your worries with someone that you trust. Get their ideas and help.

Draw a picture of the things that make you feel worried.

Help yourself to feel less worried about a big event by practising as much as you can.

Glossary

bullying when a person harms or is nasty to somebody

concentrate focus all your attention on something, so that you can do it properly

explain describe something in a way that makes it easier to understand

feeling something that happens inside our minds. It can affect our bodies and the way we behave.

nervous scared or worried about doing something

Find out more

Books

All Kinds of Feelings: A Lift-the-Flap Book, Emma Brownjohn (Tango Books, 2003)

The Huge Bag of Worries, Virginia Ironside (Hodder Children's Books, 2011)

Wemberly Worried, Kevin Henkes (HarperCollins, 2010)

Websites

bbc.co.uk/scotland/education/health/feelings

kidshealth.org/kid/feeling

pbskids.org/arthur/games/aboutface

Index